Little
Pebble™
T0081110
Colorful Foods
CAPSTONE PRESS
a capstone imprint

Little Pebble is published by Capstone Press,
1710 Roe Crest Drive, North Mankato, Minnesota 56003
www.mycapstone.com

Copyright © 2017 by Capstone Press, a Capstone imprint. All rights reserved. No part of this publication may be reproduced in whole or in part, or stored in a retrieval system, or transmitted in any form or by any means, electronic, mechanical, photocopying, recording, or otherwise, without written permission of the publisher.

Library of Congress Cataloging-in-Publication Data
Names: Rustad, Martha E. H. (Martha Elizabeth Hillman), 1975– author.
Title: Red foods / by Martha E. H. Rustad.
Description: North Mankato, Minnesota : Capstone Press, [2017] | Audience: Ages 4–7. | Audience: K to grade 3. | Includes bibliographical references and index.
Identifiers: LCCN 2016009743|
ISBN 9781515723738 (library binding)
ISBN 9781515723776 (paperback)
ISBN 9781515723813 (ebook pdf)
Subjects: LCSH: Food--Juvenile literature. | Red—Juvenile literature. | Color of food—Juvenile literature.
Classification: LCC TX355 .R856 2017 | DDC 641.3—dc23
LC record available at http://lccn.loc.gov/2016009743

Editorial Credits
Megan Atwood, editor; Juliette Peters, designer;
Jo Miller, media researcher; Steve Walker, production specialist

Photo Credits
Images by Capstone Studio: Karon Dubke
Photo styling: Sarah Schuette and Marcy Morin

Printed and bound in the United States of America.
756

Table of Contents

Red Foods 4

Red Fruits 6

Red Vegetables 14

Red Meals 18

Glossary 22

Read More 23

Internet Sites 23

Index 24

Red Foods

What does the color
red taste like?
Let's think of red foods.

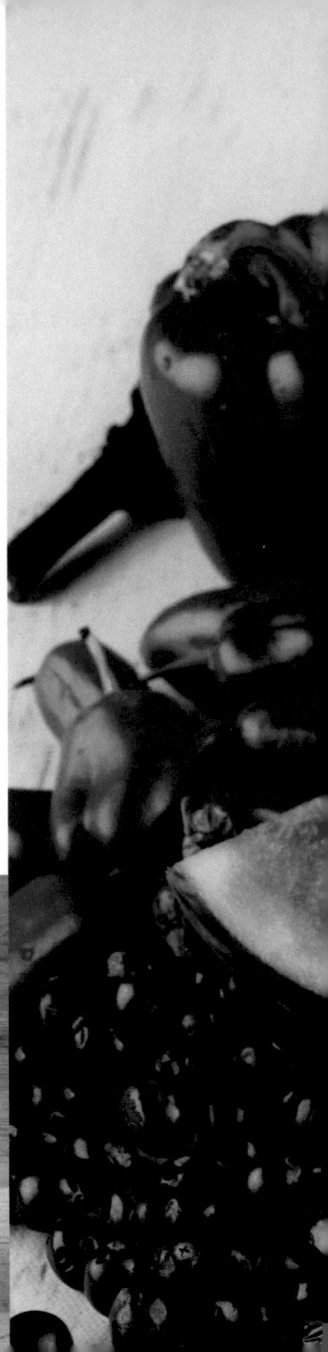

Red Fruits

Red apples are ripe.

Crunch!

Apples taste tart.

A watermelon grows

on a vine.

The inside is red.

Strawberries smell sweet.

Sniff!

We make jam.

Yum!

Cherries are juicy.

They have pits.

Red Vegetables

Red potatoes have red skin.

Dig them up to eat.

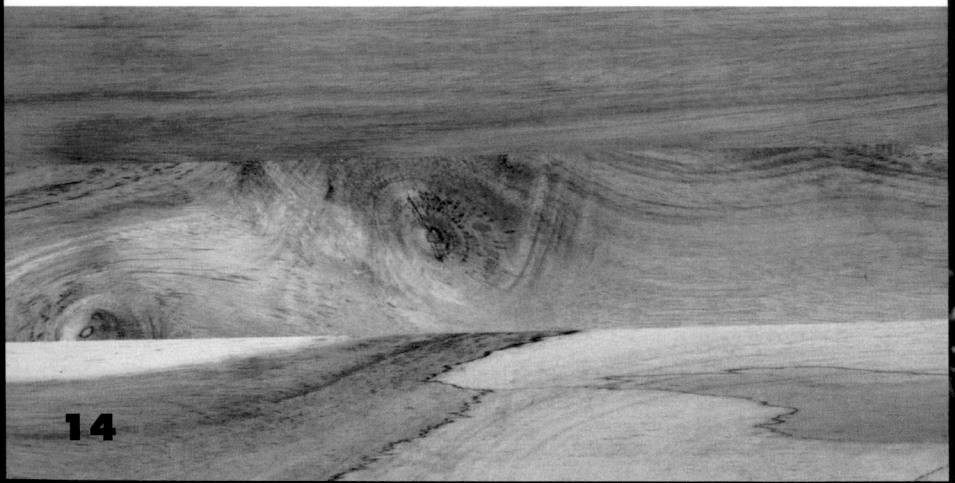

Red peppers grow in a garden.

A red bell pepper is mild.

Red chili peppers are spicy.

bell peppers
chili peppers

Red Meals

My uncle cooks red
beans and rice.
It's my favorite meal!

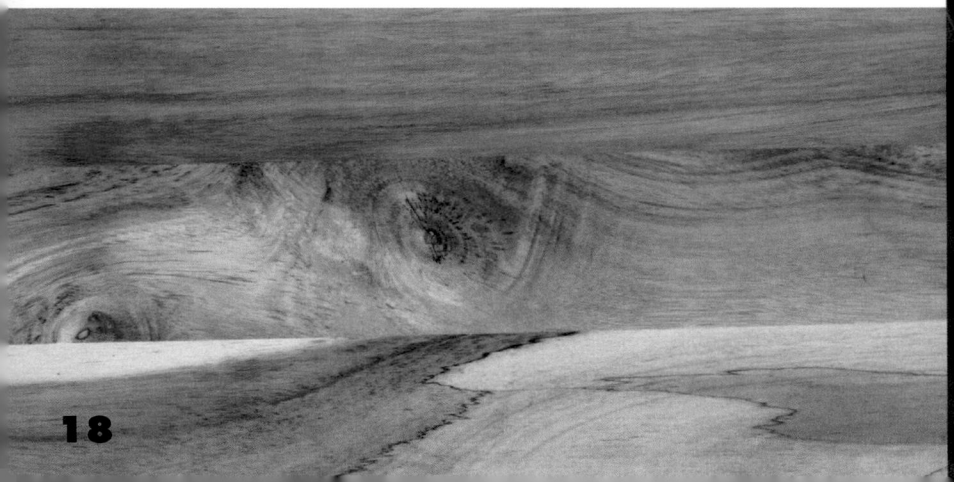

We eat pasta for lunch.

Tomatoes make the sauce red.

What other foods are red?

Glossary

jam—a sweet, thick spread made with sugar and fruit

mild—a flavor that is gentle in the mouth

pasta—a food made from flour and water

pit—a seed inside some fruits

sauce—a thick liquid eaten with food

spicy—having a strong flavor that feels hot in the mouth

tart—a flavor that tastes a little sour

vine—the stem of fruits or vegetables that grow along the ground

Read More

Glaser, Rebecca Stromstad. *Red.* Colors in Nature. Minneapolis: Bullfrog Books, 2014.

Heos, Bridget. *So You Want to Grow a Pizza?* Grow Your Food. Mankato, Minn.: Amicus, 2016.

Nunn, Daniel. *Red.* Colors All Around Us. Chicago: Heinemann-Raintree, 2012.

Internet Sites

FactHound offers a safe, fun way to find Internet sites related to this book. All of the sites on FactHound have been researched by our staff.

Here's all you do:
Visit *www.facthound.com*
Type in this code: 9781515723738

Index

apples, 6
cherries, 12
jam, 10
pasta, 20
pits, 12
red beans and rice, 18
red chili peppers, 16
red peppers, 16
red potatoes, 14
ripe, 6
sauce, 20
strawberries, 10
tomatoes, 20
vine, 8
watermelon, 8